Perfect
JERSEY

ANDY STANSFIELD

HALSGROVE

First published in Great Britain in 2008

Frontispiece photograph: *Hamptonne Country Life Museum.*

British Library Cataloguing-in-Publication Data
A CIP record for this title is available from the British Library

ISBN 978 1 84114 720 8

HALSGROVE
Halsgrove House
Ryelands Industrial Estate
Bagley Road, Wellington,
Somerset TA21 9PZ
Tel: 01823 653777
Fax: 01823 216796
email: sales@halsgrove.com
website: www.halsgrove.com

Printed and bound by D'Auria Grafiche Flaminia, Italy

INTRODUCTION

Jersey is an odd place. Or to be more precise, it is a peculiar place. Quite literally, as it is what is known as a Crown Peculiar. Although it has long since pledged allegiance to the throne it is not part of the UK, nor is it a colony or one of the overseas territories. However it is owned by the Crown, its citizens hold British passports, and its laws are ultimately dependent upon Westminster. By and large it has been allowed the freedom to govern itself but that freedom could, theoretically, be withdrawn at any time. Jersey's official status is that of a Crown Dependency but it has its own parliament known as the States of Jersey.

The island issues its own banknotes which are backed by the Bank of England and have the Queen's head on them, yet Jersey banknotes are not legal tender in the UK. However, this does not mean that they cannot be used for transactions – simply that both parties must agree upon their use. (Credit cards, for example, are not classed as legal tender either.) In practice, however, you would be hard pressed to find a travel agent who would change Jersey banknotes for English ones because they aren't listed as foreign currency either.

Then there's the French connection. Driving on the left whilst passing side roads which all have French names is quite confusing at first. Many of the place names retain a French element, including the use of accents some of the time, yet the island's day to day life centres on its twelve parishes, most of which have quintessentially English names like St John, St Lawrence and so on. Meanwhile the telephone directory takes away any doubt about Jersey's French heritage once you look down the list of surnames. So Jersey owes a great deal of its history to Norman influences and its own patois, known as Jèrriais, is based upon Norman French. More recently, families from Brittany used to visit as seasonal workers, picking potatoes for example, so there is a Breton influence too. Today Jèrriais is a form which is still widely spoken in the homes of older Jersey families but which is less well known in its written guise.

However, if you hear a foreign language being spoken in the street, in a hotel or café among the staff, it is as likely to be Polish as anything else. The island has a huge number of Polish young people working in all manner of jobs but especially the catering industry and some of the old restrictions about length of stay have been lifted so that you'll now encounter Poles who have lived on the island for years.

It will come as no surprise, then, that 'A Sense of Identity' is the working title of the first chapter of a follow-up book on Jersey. What continues to surprise me every time I visit the island is the number of layers of history which can be peeled back by choosing to talk with local people from differing family backgrounds.

Scenic Jersey is equally diverse. For such a small area, roughly 45 square miles, the range of subject matter for artists and photographers to capture is out of all proportion to its size. To give a graphic example, I have recently returned from a two-week visit with around 2000 images to download onto my computer. What's more, the variations in light – especially at sunset – mean that you can easily justify visiting certain locations again and again. Consequently, you will find that some locations appear several times on these pages.

In the preparation of this book I have been assisted by many people. Particular thanks must go to Jersey Tourism for both their direct support and for putting me in touch with many Jersey residents, ranging from farmers to fishermen, artisans to archivists, all of whom I found eager to share their experiences and opinions, and I owe a debt of gratitude to them all.

Andy Stansfield

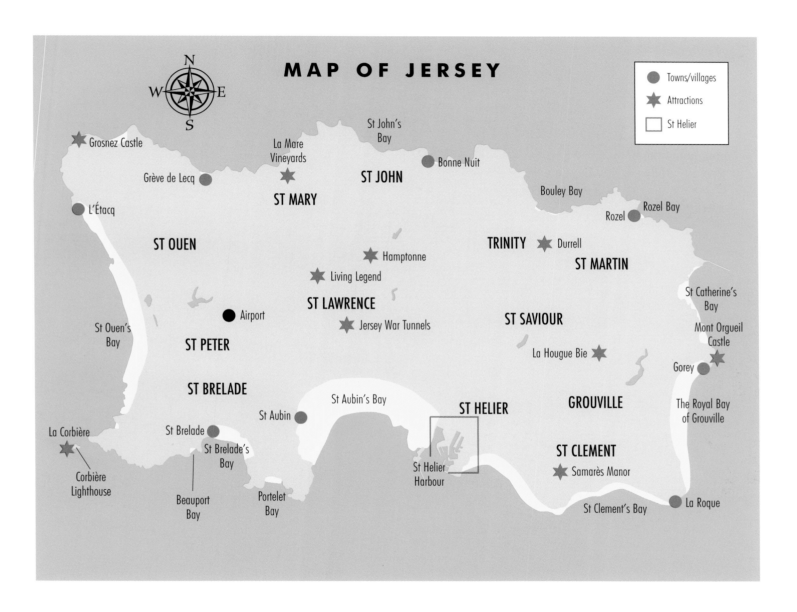

MAP OF JERSEY

Towns/villages
Attractions
St Helier

Grosnez Castle
Grève de Lecq
L'Étacq
St John's Bay
La Mare Vineyards
ST JOHN
Bonne Nuit
ST MARY
Bouley Bay
Rozel
Rozel Bay
ST OUEN
TRINITY
Durrell
Hamptonne
ST MARTIN
Living Legend
St Catherine's Bay
St Ouen's Bay
Airport
ST LAWRENCE
Jersey War Tunnels
ST SAVIOUR
Mont Orgueil Castle
ST PETER
La Hougue Bie
Gorey
La Corbière
ST BRELADE
St Aubin's Bay
ST HELIER
GROUVILLE
The Royal Bay of Grouville
Corbière Lighthouse
St Brelade
St Aubin
St Helier Harbour
St Brelade's Bay
ST CLEMENT
Samarès Manor
Beauport Bay
Portelet Bay
St Clement's Bay
La Roque

Hamptonne
This splendid country life museum is operated by the National Trust for Jersey.

La Roque

One of the author's favourite locations, La Roque can be found in the south-east of the island and offers
a wide variety of photographic opportunities at all times of the day and whatever the state of the tide.
In this shot a lone fishing boat balances the composition.

Jersey's main attractions
These two shots have been carefully chosen to introduce Jersey's key attractions: rugged splendour, dramatic skies, a sense of history, and the colourful interpretation of it by island residents for the benefit of visitors.

Falconry at Mont Orgueil Castle
Further photos of Sue Headon and her birds can be found on pages 47-49.
Left: a jagged granite outcrop in the south-west corner of the island contrasts with a moody early evening sky.

La Hougue Bie

This is one of the most important archaeological sites in Europe, consisting of a huge burial mound dating from 3800 BC within which lies a Neolithic passage grave. Every equinox a small group of people can visit at sunrise to see the sun light up the chamber, weather permitting.

On top of the mound lie two medieval chapels. An elegant folly called the Prince's Tower was added to the chapels at the end of the eighteenth century but was pulled down in 1924.

La Pouquelaye de Faldouet

Another impressive antiquity in the area is the dolmen at Faldouet, a splendid example that is difficult to visit as it lies off a single-track road with no parking even remotely near it.

Sean Falkner and spider crab
If you find yourself eating seafood on the island, there's a strong possibility it was supplied
by Faulkner Fisheries based at L'Étacq. Sean Faulkner is seen here with one of the huge
spider crabs which are caught by the island's low-water fishermen.

Gravy boat by Rosemary Blackmore
A locally crafted ceramic gravy boat on display at the Harbour Gallery in St Aubin.

Succulent ground cover near Kempt Tower
This exotic ground cover plant stretched thirty feet over sand dunes near Kempt Tower.
Sand dunes are also a habitat for the green lizard, Jersey being the only place in Britain to see our largest
and most spectacular lizard in its natural habitat – if you are lucky. Fewer than 4000 are left in the wild.

A surprising find
Honeysuckle growing in a cliff-top location on the south coast.

Pampas grass and seed pods
With clear blue skies it is possible to juxtapose all kinds of combinations to come up with a stunning photo.

The Red Arrows
The UK's best known air display
specialists performing at an air show
above St Aubin's Bay give airline
passengers a bird's eye view –
and possibly a bit of a surprise.

17

Autumn colour
Even in autumn, as here, the gardens along the promenade at St Brelade offer a splendid display.

Jersey's most famous car

Another feast for the eyes, Bergerac's car can be found on display at the entrance to Jersey Goldsmiths at Lion Park.

One of the island's islands
The pyramid-shaped island of L'île Percée at the entrance to Portelet Bay.

An architectural oddity
'Seagull' is an oddly designed property resembling a boat and can be found on the dunes of St Ouen's Bay.

Nature's palette
Opportunities abound for colourful and contrasting subject matter, whether it's
Navelwort growing on a granite wall or shells in a rock pool.

Photography tip

Rocks and pebbles need to be wet to bring out their full colour so carry a small
bottle of water with you. You can always refill it in a rock pool.

Rock and sky
Dramatic close-up of a granite outcrop at La Roque set against a deep blue sky.
The clearest skies and deepest blues usually follow the passage of a weather front.

Kempt Tower

This Jersey round tower (actually it's slightly elliptical) on St Ouen's Bay houses a visitor centre.

Bountiful Jersey

The island is synonymous with agricultural produce, especially its dairy products and famous Jersey Royal potatoes. Less well-known is the La Mare Wine Estate which cultivates both grapes and apples for its wine and cider (opposite). Individual farmers growing and selling vegetables direct to the public, however, are few and far between now as large collectives have taken over. Didier Helio (opposite) of Manor Farm in St Ouen's is one of the few farmers who have bucked the trend. He grows a wide range of vegetables including some odd varieties such as black carrots.

Unexpected encounter

This atmospheric gateway was stumbled upon on a ninety degree bend on a single track road somewhere in the centre of the island – the author was completely lost at the time. Route-finding on Jersey can best be described as interesting and even locals with generations of family history on the island frequently admit to losing their way.

Political comment

This is the most impressive set of gates the author found on the island, with two small cannon set behind them, and with the residence so far down the drive it wasn't visible. They belong to the Residence du Consul General Republique Rwandaise. Quite why one of Africa's poorer countries needs a consulate at all on Jersey, let alone such a lavish property, is a mystery.

The war remembered
Above and opposite: scenes from the Channel Islands Military Museum, situated adjacent to Lewis's Tower on St Ouen's Bay.
A compact museum set in a bunker, there are fascinating displays of island life under German occupation.

La Roque at high tide
The free car park, clean toilets and small snack bar make this a favourite spot for visitors and locals alike.

Contre jour

La Corbière lighthouse taken from the causeway moments before it was completely covered by the incoming tide.

Seasonal colour
Spring is the best time to visit Jersey
for its gardens but autumn presents
a colourful show too.

Fruit feature
An attractive tunnel created by apple trees at Samarès Manor.

35

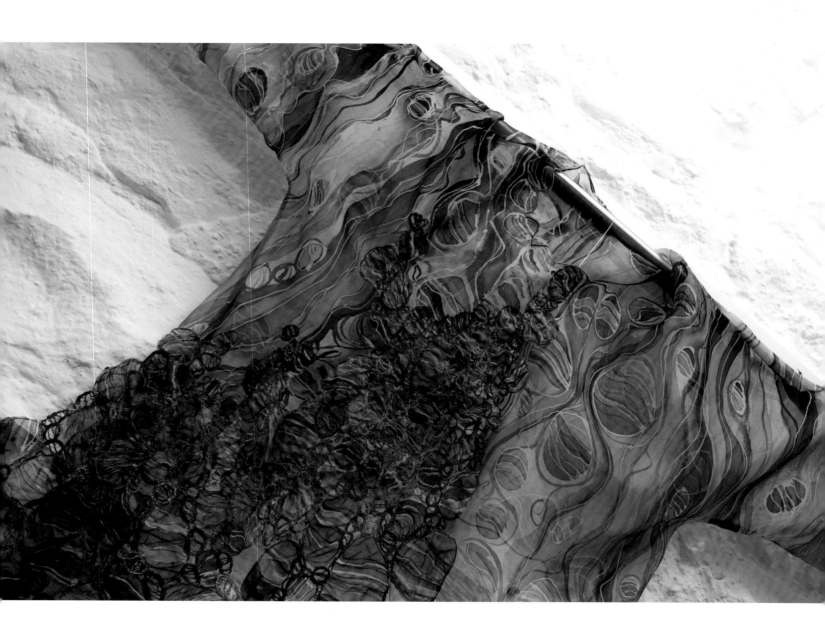

Local crafts
Above: Driftwood heart necklace
created by Natalie Moss.

Right: Reproduction Hepplewhite chair from 1852
by Remi Couriard who, as well as creating stylish
wooden furniture, leads Gourmet Walks on the
island and is also a well-known Blue Badge Guide.

Opposite: Delicate blouse made
of silk organza by Di Richardson.

Genuine Jersey
The Harbour Gallery on the quayside at St Aubin
is a major centre for artists and craftsmen working
on the island. All the items here were part of a
special Genuine Jersey exhibition. Genuine Jersey
exists to promote the crafts, food products and
agricultural produce of a wide range of
members on the island.

Surf safety
Lifeguards at Le Braye on the sweeping sands of St Ouen's Bay, one of a number of island
beaches which are regularly patrolled to ensure safe bathing, surfing and kayaking.

La Saline slip
L'Étacq from the slipway at La Saline, St Ouen's Bay.

St Brelade

Above and opposite: St Brelade's Parish Church and Fishermen's Chapel at night. The shot opposite also shows the lights along the promenade of St Brelade reflected off the still-wet beach shortly after high tide.

Castle ruins
Very little remains of Grosnez Castle, perched on dramatic cliffs in the north-west corner of the island, but the ruins do offer some interesting angles.

Jersey War Tunnels

This is one of the island's most popular attractions and a thorough visit should allow two to three hours.
Over one kilometre of tunnels, hewn out of the rock by forced labour from across Europe during the German occupation,
houses exhibits focusing on the experiences of local people during the occupation. The entrance ticket is in the form
of an identity card from the period. This chilling shot shows the operating theatre in the Underground Hospital.

Battery Moltke

A German gun emplacement above L'Étacq at the Battery Moltke. Whilst here the author bumped into Billy Burt, a local who had experienced the occupation as a lad, and spent a fascinating hour listening to tales of one-upmanship as Billy recalled the ways in which teenagers risked punishment by 'getting one over on the Jerries'.

Landmark

This Jersey National Trust-owned eighteenth-century powder magazine is affectionately known variously as Le Don Hilton,
the white house or the white hut. Its proper title is La Caumine à Marie Best. Originally a guardhouse,
it was rebuilt in 1765 and today serves as a stark landmark for shipping.

Wilhelmina

This stunning bird of prey is a Ferruginous eagle native to the USA and captive bred in the UK. She can be seen taking part in falconry displays at Mont Orgueil Castle. For the record her optimum flying weight is 3lb 4oz.

Family portrait
Falconry at Mont Orgueil Castle with Sue Headon (aka Lady Anne Heydon
when she is working) in period costume with Wilhelmina.

Expressions

Above: Sue Headon with Sky, a three year old Bay-winged hawk native to Mexico and also bred in the UK. Sue's hands often mirror the bird's wing movements during the display.

Left: Wilhelmina making her feelings known.

Le Saut Geoffroi
Slipway at this small cove just north of Gorey.

Composition

Sandy coves normally provide sweeping curves with which to work, so it was a pleasant change to experiment with the straight lines on offer here.

Shades of green
Jersey's favourable climate means
that huge varieties of tree shapes
and colours can be found.

Shades of Kent
Normally associated with the county reputed to be the 'garden of England' these hops were found growing on the south coast of the island.

Round towers and forts

Top right: Le Hocq – the seaward side of many towers is often painted white to aid shipping.

Bottom right: Royal Jersey Golf Club and Fort Henry.

Left and opposite: Lewis's Tower, next to the Channel Islands Military Museum, on St Ouen's Bay.

Fortified Jersey

As defences against the French in the late eighteenth and early nineteenth centuries,
numerous fortified towers were constructed around Jersey's coastline, of which 24 remain.

Samarès Manor
Guided tours of the Manor House and its Carriage and Farm Vehicle Museum take place several times a day but visitors can wander its grounds and themed gardens at will.

Sacred Heart
The dramatic outline of this Roman
Catholic church can't be missed as you
approach St Aubin from St Helier.

Freedom
The seafront cycle path between St Aubin and St Helier is not just a useful recreational facility – it is
also a popular commuting option, avoiding peak traffic into and out of St Helier, where most residents work.

Admiring the view
May is a popular time to visit Jersey and the Spring Walking Festival provides a chance to walk the entire coastline in stages with transport provided from and back to St Helier each day.

Safe haven
An atmospheric shot of boats moored off La Roque.

Sunset at La Corbière
Watching the setting sun from the car park above La Corbière lighthouse is a popular
option and the skies are never the same two days running.

Grève de Lecq
Above and opposite: The beach at Grève de Lecq on the north coast is a firm favourite for family outings to the beach, kayaking, snorkelling and launching small boats.

Nostalgia
Remember the days when AA members used to be issued a key for these boxes and when patrolmen used to salute motorists who proudly displayed their AA badge on their radiator grille?

Ouaisné Bay

A much simpler rescue and recovery operation is needed for sand yachting on the beach at Ouaisné Bay. At the eastern end of the bay is a headland from which woolly mammoths used to be driven to their deaths on the rocks below.

Bonne Nuit
Above and opposite: Mooring chains on the beach at Bonne Nuit provide graphic subject matter.

Shocking pink
Above and opposite: Pelargoniums at Rozel provide a vivid splash of colour.

St Aubin
The cobbles and pastel colours of High Street are a worthwhile diversion from the seafront.

Rozel harbour
These steps at the side of
the jetty at Rozel, leading down
into the depths at high tide,
make a colourful composition.

71

Eye catching
This lichen-encrusted rock on the south coast held a strange attraction.

L'île Agois

Viewed here from the north coast cliff path, L'île Agois revealed the remains of several circular dwellings during archaeological excavations in the mid 1970s. It is thought that these may have belonged to a small group of hermit monks.

Hamptonne Country Life Museum
Set in the island's heartland,
Hamptonne is set in a farm complex
and staff in period costume lend
an air of authenticity.

Sadie Renard
As well as working at Hamptonne, Sadie is well known as the semi-official singer of the island's anthem 'Beautiful Jersey'.

La Corbière

Variations on a theme
Two versions of a sunset at La Corbière emphasising the warmer colours in one and the colder colours in the other.

Jersey Lavender

Alastair Christie worked in the chemical industry as a specialist in perfumes until he took over his parents' lavender farm.
Now he breathes the heady aroma of lavender all day long. As well as seven fields of lavender, there are attractive gardens to walk
around and a talk which explains how the lavender is distilled and used for a variety of products which are on sale in the shop.

Noirmont Point
This gun emplacement on the headland between St Aubin's Bay and
Portelet Bay is a permanent platform for a 15cm SK L/45 naval gun.

Le Petit Port
It's not often that seagulls are co-operative but this one stayed still long enough for a
sequence of shots at the small bay of Le Petit Port at the southern end of St Ouen's Bay.

St Brelade's Bay at dusk
Dramatic bands of light and shadow on the beach are caught in the last moments before the sun drops below the horizon.

Moods of La Corbière
Shafts of sunlight through the clouds and patches of light reflected off the sea turn this silhouette into something magical.

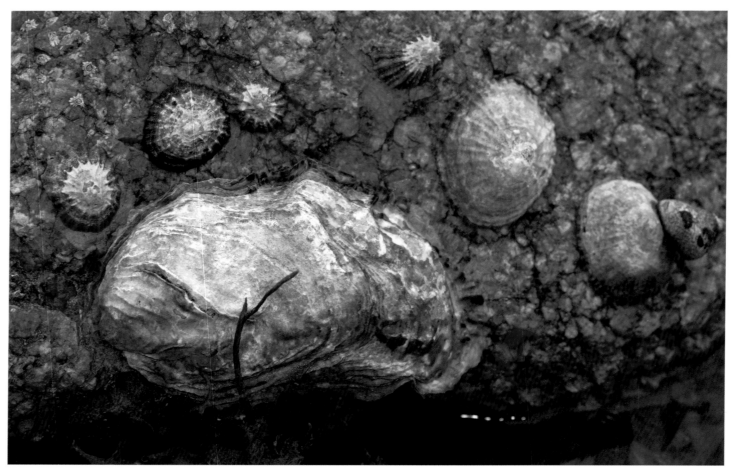

Limpets and oyster on granite

Sounds like an item on the menu and, actually, that's not far from the truth. Many Jersey residents tell tales of how, as children, they were sent down to the beach by their mothers to find something in the rock pools for lunch.

Field gateway on the road to Beauport Bay

Morel Farm, St Lawrence

This Jersey National Trust-owned farmhouse was constructed by the Langlois family in the same year as the Great Fire of London but it was later acquired by the Morel family, hence its present name. It has an impressive archway entrance, an unusual cobbled courtyard, and a pressoir where apples were crushed and cider was made.

Arched gateway and fuschias
This lovely gateway leads from the walled garden to the less formal gardens and grounds of Samarès Manor.

Colombier

Also at Samarès Manor is this colombier or dovecote. Built as a circular tower, the nesting holes are only visible from inside. Colombiers such as this only occur within the grounds of manors owned by the Seigneur of a fief. Two square colombiers can also be found on Jersey, the first being at Hamptonne Country Life Museum and the second at La Haule in St Brelade.

Cart and flowers, Grouville Bay
A touch of French influence is found in this display along the coast road near the island's eastern shore.

Karting at the Jersey Experience

Most adrenaline sports are beach-based but karting can be tried on a dedicated track at Jersey Experience, also home to the Living Legend multi-sensory show which documents the island's past.

Breaking surf
Westerly winds produce rolling breakers in La Baie à Sablion.

Harbour, St Aubin
Opting to shoot when the boats in the foreground were under a cloud shadow
meant less contrast so the greens of the hillside could be retained.

Rocks at La Roque

The emphasis on the foreground and the two boats in the middle distance give this shot a great sense of depth. To create depth in a photo it is better to have several distinct planes of interest rather than having a subject which continually recedes into the distance. This works much better than it would have done at low tide when La Roque's 'moonscape' of low water rocks would have filled the area occupied by the sea.

Rocks and surf

La Maison Maret

To be found next to Holy Trinity Parish Church in Trinity village, this fabulous residence is one of Jersey's real gems.

Royal Jersey Golf Club
Adjacent to the sands of Grouville Bay, golfers play a round with Mont Orgueil Castle on the skyline.

Horse riding on country lane
Jersey has a maximum speed limit of just 40mph but there is also a network of lanes with a
limit of only 15mph to facilitate increased safety for cyclists, walkers and horse riders.

Seat with a view

Wherever there is a fine view there is usually a bench so you can sit and enjoy it. The other thing that is noticeable when touring the island is the frequency of excellently maintained public toilets.

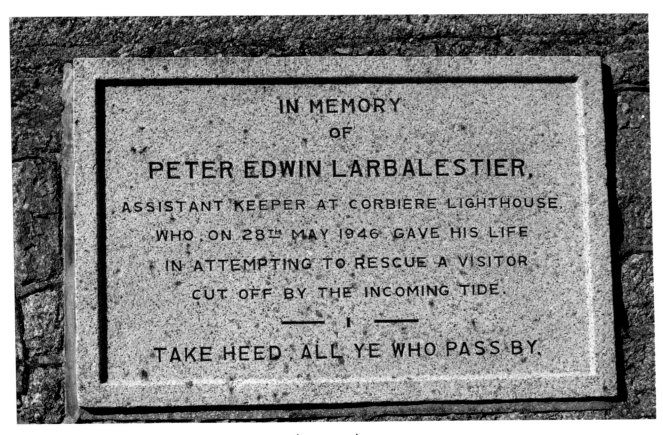

In memoriam
Assistant lighthouse keeper Peter Larbalestier is remembered for his sacrifice in trying to save a visitor who was caught out by the incoming tide. Jersey's tidal reach is one of the highest in the world and can rise at the rate of 10ft in an hour.

Bird's eye view
The jetty at Bonne Nuit photographed from high above on the north coast cliff path.

Lone kayak

A single canoeist off Grève de Lecq explores the north coast. There are numerous opportunities for kayak instruction and guided trips to offshore locations.

Abstract
An upturned boat on the jetty at Gorey harbour.

This way

Durrell

Often referred to as Jersey Zoo, Durrell is actually a very different kind of enterprise. It was established by Gerald Durrell (see bronze statue on right) as a sanctuary and breeding centre in 1959 and became the headquarters of the Durrell Wildlife Conservation Trust in 1963. It is a worldwide organisation dedicated to saving animals from extinction. For example, there are white Bali starlings being bred here because there are fewer than two dozen left in the wild. Each exhibit has a display board indicating its threat level, location and notes on the species: two enormous Burmese pythons, we are informed, are generally quite placid... if treated with caution and respect. As if we would do otherwise.

The gorillas are a firm favourite with visitors and provide hours of entertainment with their antics, expressions and body language. They even adorn the walls of the restaurant.

Low tide at Le Hocq
The tide recedes far enough to allow careful, and preferably guided, walkers to go out to Icho and Seymour Towers.
White-painted Icho can be seen in the far distance just right of centre. It is also possible to stay overnight on
Seymour Tower while the tide rises forty feet around you, an experience billed as the 'Moonwalk' which has
more to do with the lunar landscape you cross at low tide than the overnight element.

Artist at work

Local resident Paul O'Flaherty painting at Gorey harbour. Paul is one of a number of professional artists to be found living in Jersey and one of very few who work almost entirely on location.

Jersey Pottery

Expecting a quaint cottage industry, the author admits to being caught out by the sheer scale of Jersey Pottery's operation, set in the heart of Gorey village. It is possible to view the craftsmen at work and there is a huge shop selling an extensive range which makes it ideal for choosing a present for someone back home.

Seaweed and slip

Sometimes it is possible to just look down at your feet and there is a photograph waiting to be captured.

Sense of scale

The distant ship gives some idea of the size of target this German 15cm gun would have had to aim at.

Bonsai
These two bonsai trees in the gardens of Samarès Manor are fine examples of the art.

Beauport Bay

Of the dozens of bays and coves on the island, this is one of the least publicised and one of the author's favourites. It is accessed by a long set of steps from the car park high above. At the back of the beach is a bank of large smooth pink granite boulders and the beach itself is broken by an attractive cluster of rocks. In the middle distance the red granite stack picks up added colour from the setting sun.

North Coast Scenery
With sunny weather and no air pollution, vibrant natural colours are the order of the day.

Green
Coastal path steps leading to
the cliff top car park between
Bonne Nuit and Bouley Bay.

Red
This humorous weather station at Rozel indicates a windy day.

Stripes
Getting ready for a day's sailing at the Royal Channel Islands Yacht Club base
near the Gunsite Café, half way along St Aubin's Bay.

Deserted beach, Rozel

Even the occupiers of the travel rug seem to have left the scene. The island's beaches are often quiet regardless of the season.

En route
Footpaths, especially around the coast, are clearly marked and easy to follow. If only the same could be said of the maze of country lanes which constitutes the island's heartland!

Giffard Bay
View westwards across
Giffard Bay towards Rozel.

Trinity Parish Church

Jersey is divided into 12 parishes and the social importance of these remains far greater than is the case on the UK mainland. Some parishes have a well-defined village at their heart, like St John's. Others lack a focal point as they consist of a scattering of small hamlets and farms. Despite this, parish activities like amateur dramatics draw people together and a great sense of rivalry exists between parishes. The author once ventured to suggest that the Channel Islands as a whole would benefit from marketing themselves collectively. 'How can we do that,' replied the local resident, 'when we can't even get the parishes to agree on anything?'

Autumn colour
The green and gold shades of a crab apple tree contrast with the fading blues of hydrangeas.

The cat's whiskers
This scone with locally made jam and fresh Jersey cream lasted long enough to be photographed – but only just.

Sedum, Rozel

Ground cover plants in Jersey seem to thrive and this carpet of sedum in flower is no exception.

Steps at Gorey harbour

Seafront shelter tiled roof

Off the beaten track
While the harbours, quayside pubs and beach cafés of seaside towns will always attract the most visitors it is always worth exploring the back streets to discover buildings with a history, like this cottage in St Aubin which dates back to 1694.

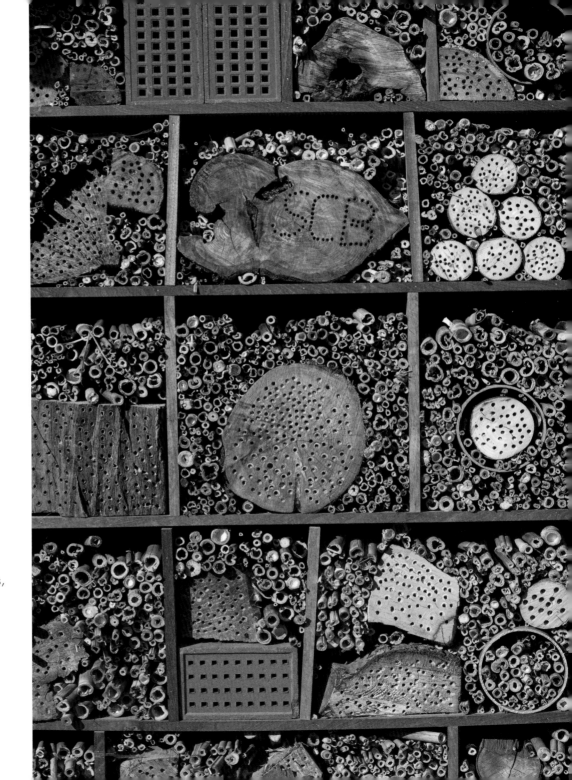

Insect tower, Durrell
Providing a home for a wide
variety of insect life which in turn
encourages a wider variety of birds,
insect towers like this are easy to
make and are becoming an
increasingly common sight.

Yellow and blue
These two 'cottages' opposite the harbour at Rozel add a splash of colour even on dull days.

Seafront binoculars on the promenade at Gorey.

Lone seagull

This gull appears to be doing nothing more than staring out to sea, so perhaps it's not just us who are captivated by seascapes.

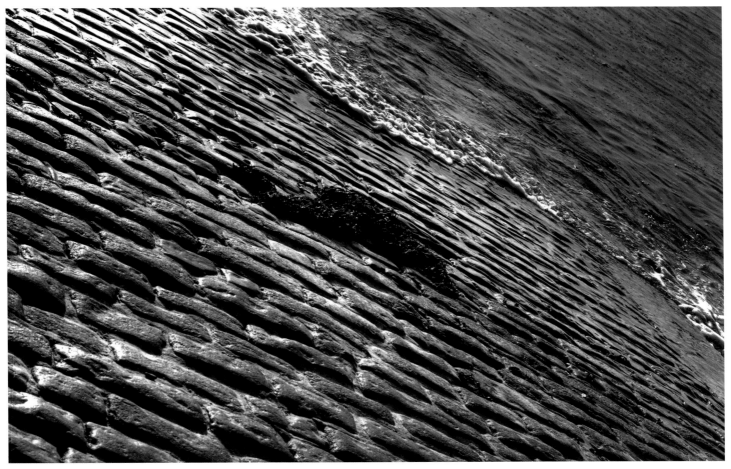

Seaweed and slip
Diagonal lines always add drama to a shot. Sometimes it's as simple as rotating the camera,
as with this image captured at Le Hocq.

Tribute

These clasped hands, symbolising one person pulling another to safety, are an evocative monument of thanks for the rescue of the French ferry *Saint Malo* which struck the rocks of Le Frouquie nearly a kilometre north of La Corbière during Force 5 seas in April 1995. With the prompt aid of emergency services and nearby shipping, all 307 passengers and crew were rescued safely.

Pallot Steam Museum

Tucked away in the countryside, this museum contains an extensive collection of transport exhibits of all kinds and even has its own short stretch of railway track.

Water feature
Every Spring many private homes open their gardens to the public.
Full details can be obtained from the tourist board's website.

Apple crush

This granite apple crusher consists of a stone wheel which rotates along a circular channel which is filled with apples during the initial stages of cider making. This one happens to be outside but others can be found inside a pressoir, a building which would also have held presses and vats, such as that at the National Trust-owned Morel Farm in St Lawrence.

Dusk over St Ouen's Bay

La Rocco Tower
Shown on the Ordnance Survey map as La Tour de la Rocque-Ho but more familiarly known as La Rocco Tower, it stands off-shore at Le Braye on St Ouen's Bay and is a favourite spot for kite-surfing at sunset.

Mont Orgueil Castle and Gorey
The castle has variously been called Castrum de Gurri, Le Château de Gouray, Castellum de Gurrit and Chastel de Mountorguylle. The spelling of Gorey (still sometimes Gouray) has had many variations including Gorroic, Gorryk and Gourroic.